Self Defense Made Simple:

Easy and Effective Self Protection Whatever Your Age, Size or Skill!

Phil Pierce

Copyright © 2014

www.BlackBeltFit.com

This publication (and any by this Author) may not be copied or reproduced in any format, by any means - electronic or otherwise - without prior consent from the copyright owner or publisher.

All content Copyright © 2014.

All content herein is considered a guide only.

No liability is accepted for the practice of Martial Arts, Self Defense, fitness or any other activity.

What Can You Get From This Book?

- Do you want to learn how to ensure you <u>never get hit</u> using one special technique?

- Or how to use psychology 'hacks' to prevent violence before it happens and stay in control?

- Learn how to <u>really</u> use everyday objects as weapons (90% of people get this wrong!)

- Discover the truth behind pressure points – and how you can use them

- How to defend yourself against the most common attacks

- How to use the powerful self-defense tools your body already has

- Learn the exact exercises you can use to quickly and easily build a 'self-defense body'

- How to find the weak points on an attacker…that you can exploit!

- How to choose the perfect self-defense class (and which ones are just wasting your time)

- Understand how to identify a threat before it ever happens

- How to avoid the No.1, life-threatening self-defense mistake

And more!

This book is your blueprint for smarter, easier and more intuitive self-protection without the years of training or complicated lessons.

Based on the tactics of Self-Defense experts, top Martial Artists and security personnel the simple techniques included are all designed to enable you to stay safe on the streets whatever your age, size or skill!

Ever wondered what it takes in a real life or death situation to make the right choices? Or how to dominate any violent encounter on the streets without even throwing a punch? You may be surprised at the answers...

Contents

Free Bonus Book!

Grab your Completely Free bonus book;
'How to Develop Power with Plyometrics' now!

Just head over to my site:

www.BlackBeltFit.com

Claim your copy now!

From the Author

I was humbled by the amazing reception of my bestselling self-defense book 'How to Defend Yourself in 3 Seconds or Less', and a lot of people have told me how useful they have found it. I'm incredibly happy that it has helped people of all ages and abilities better reduce the chance of being a victim no matter where they live. I soon realized however, that I had a lot more to offer people who wanted to better understand the practical aspects of Self Defense.

'Self Defense Made Simple' is all about making self-protection easy and accessible for you – regardless of your age, ability, or fitness level!

Many people instantly find excuses for not working out or maintaining an exercise routine and go on to assume that similar rules apply to self-protection.

"I'm too old"
"I'm too weak"
"I'm smaller than others"

The good news for you is that self-defense is 90% brain and 10% body. In other words; if you can fight smart you might not have to fight at all!

Most people don't want to spend years training or learning a martial art, so this book is about developing a better understanding of avoiding violence using firstly your brain and then your body to react if you can't.

But even if you have learned a traditional style, I guarantee you will learn some eye-opening approaches to self-defense.

As always, it's crucial to understand that self-defense is not about learning techniques with which to beat someone up. In fact, using violence is the very last resort and should be considered only if all the other steps have failed. If you are looking for "street fighting" methods or techniques for beating people up, I suggest you look elsewhere. (Perhaps a therapist!)

What you will find in this guide are powerful tactics for handling any dangerous encounter quickly and easily. Including;

- How to avoid ever getting hit
- How to use everyday objects in self-defense
- Which targets you should choose on an opponent
- The awesome self-defense tools you already have (but might not know about!)
- How to identify a threat before it ever happens
- The truth behind Pressure points

And much more!

Foreword: Principle Before Practice

You may be keen to skip straight to the actual techniques and learn how to start taking out muggers, rapists, or anyone that looks at you funny, but wait just a moment.

I wanted to include a selection of the actual strikes and physical target zones because I think it's important to balance the practical and theoretical. I can't stress enough though how important a deep understanding of the principles behind self-defense are BEFORE you ever tackle any physical tactics.

Consider these principles your foundation for self-defense. Without a solid base of understanding, your physical actions will likely be shaky and unpredictable. This can make things even worse given that violence is already a pretty shaky and unpredictable experience anyway!

Ensure you have read and fully understood, on a personal level, the various chapters before believing yourself confident to face situations in the real world. It's one thing to read about adrenaline and stress affecting you, but until you truly experience it, it's common to think "Oh, that won't affect me" or "I'll be OK because I will just do X". The truth is we wouldn't *just* do anything, and it's likely we would be completely overwhelmed at the time.

I say this not to focus on the doom and gloom of the situation but to stress how important the understanding of how to use your mind and body is before you put any of it into practice.

So take a second. Look once more at the topics covered here (and elsewhere), and think about how *you* would react.

Get the Full Picture

I recommend grabbing a copy of my first Self Defense book 'How to Defend Yourself in 3 Seconds (Or Less)' to accompany this book. Not just because it's a great guide – which of course it is – but because this book builds upon many of the fundamental principles discussed in that book.

That's not to say this book won't offer distinct advantages alone, because it will. But with both guides, you can learn essential concepts of distance, positioning, and striking and really develop a deeper understanding than with one book alone.

Both guides are designed to perfectly complement each other and give you a deep and solid understanding of how to defend yourself should a bad situation arise.

Grab your copy now: http://bit.ly/1hiFSDE

Why You Should Be the "Gray" Man (or Woman!)

Some of the toughest people in the world are Special Forces soldiers, but incredibly, you'd never know it to look at them.

Military operators from the elite units like the SAS (arguably one of the originals), Delta Force, Mossad, or Spetsnaz go through grueling physical, tactical, and mental training regimes to shape them into brutal fighters capable of both armed and unarmed combat to the death.

These are the people they send into the most dangerous parts of the world to get the job done when most others would fail. So what do they look like? Muscle-bound superheroes? Shaved-headed tough guys. Camo-clad brawlers?

Actually, they look just like everyone else, and that's pretty much the point. They need to blend in, disappear, and not draw unnecessary attention to themselves to avoid danger.

I remember my father, who spent many years working in Airport security and counter terrorism, telling me about an individual he knew that had applied for British Special Forces selection. They guy was huge, muscles upon muscles, and looked like the sort who could stare down a Great White Shark.

He never made it past the first interview.

The unlucky fellow was told he stuck out like a sore thumb, had poor fitness (he couldn't run effectively due to his size), and was completely unsuitable for undercover operations.

Drawing unnecessary attention to yourself is a big no-no in top tier military or intelligence operations, and the same applies to you and I keeping safe on the street.

Sure, you may not be undercover in the back alleys of Mogadishu, but the principle for self-protection is the same. Blending in, not drawing attention to yourself, and dressing appropriately can drastically reduce the odds of you being selected as a target.

Strutting around in your MMA T-shirt and growling at anyone who passes may make you feel tough, but if a guy and his six drunk friends take offense, you are in a difficult situation no matter how strong you are.

Similarly, if ladies go out and want to dress to impress, that is fine. But walking two miles to the club in a mini-dress through the rough part of town will not end well. You stand out to everyone.

An old concept borrowed from the SAS is that of the "Grey man" (or "Gray" depending on your side of the Atlantic): Keep a low profile to blend in with the crowd and disappear. This doesn't mean you can't wear nice clothing or make an effort; it just means that you should consider how you will be perceived in your surroundings compared to the type of people and area around you.

Consider:

Moving in a crowd
This makes it hard to single out an individual.

Avoid aggressive stances
Stomping around with arms crossed, scowling at everyone will make you stick out.

Clothing
Does what you wear make any political or religious statements? Are you in bright colors while those around you aren't? Could your clothing (or lack of!) be offensive?

If you are able to minimize your visual contrast against your surroundings, whatever they are, you stand a much better chance of avoiding any danger and staying safe on the streets.

"Moves" are a Waste of Time

Although this topic was quite extensively covered in my first book 'How to Defend Yourself in 3 Seconds or Less', it bears repeating because so many people fall for the idea of watching some self-defense or martial arts video on YouTube or listening to a friend of a friend who once did Karate and instantly thinking they know what to do.

If anything this is the No.1 mistake people make when beginning to understand self-defense.

Essentially any system that tries to teach you "moves" (i.e. technical grabs and locks or special Martial Arts maneuvers for Self Defense) is probably just wasting your time. When a real-world encounter kicks off and the adrenaline destroys the smart part of your brain, anything beyond extremely simple intuitive movements will go out of the window.

That's not to say they don't have value, but many systems are designed to be practiced by a calm, rational individual training in a studio or gym. Life just isn't like that.

Let me put it to you like this. Are you a driver?

If so, do you remember what they told you at driving school about what to do if you get a blow-out at high speed? Or what to do in a car accident or emergency stop? Nope, me neither. (Incidentally, research shows that slightly accelerating is safer during a blow-out than braking, but you can read up on that one yourself.)

The simple reason we don't remember these things is because we don't want to recall unpleasant sensations. Similarly, we don't want to remember complex techniques for self-defense because we don't want to think about it and have trouble associating negative emotions with complicated movements.

Of course, you can get better at a given technique by practicing over and over, but it's surprisingly hard to simulate the effect of real-world violence on the body.

"Blocks" are a similarly flawed concept in a real world environment. Traditional Martial Arts methods involving using your forearm or palm in a specific stance or angle are far too limited for the streets. Instead, if you have to deflect an attack, we try to use the most instinctive movement to our body.

The idea behind this book is to use the most basic, primal instincts and bodily actions to avoid danger – in whatever form it takes.

Understand also that in the unlikely event you are attacked, it will be messy and awkward and probably won't go as planned, but if you can remember even one or two of the simple and intuitive tactics here and to always run when you can, you stand a much better chance.

And that might be the difference.

Self-Defense Classes – Should I Bother?

You may wonder; why bother learning any self-defense at all if real violence is so unpredictable and unnerving? The reality is that while you will likely disregard 90% of so-called training when the proverbial matter hits the fan, the 10% you do keep can be the difference between life and death.

While deciding whether to enroll in a self-defense class, you might question whether it will be worth the effort. While fairly inexpensive, most classes do come with a fee. You may also need to adjust your schedule to ensure that you can attend every class. Rest assured, this is one commitment that is worth your time and money. Participating in a self-defense class comes with countless benefits, many of which may not be initially obvious.

One of the most underestimated benefits is the confidence you will build. Your newfound strength of character is sure to affect all aspects of your life. You may find that your posture is more steady and upright. You will begin to walk with your head held tall. When a person exudes confidence, other people notice. Your boss may trust you with more responsibility or offer a promotion. You will be more likely to attract potential love matches. While the goal of these classes is to learn to defend yourself, positive changes will be obvious in everything you do, and this confidence also makes you less of a target on the street.

Additionally you will also notice your body changing. Self-defense classes can be physically demanding. In order to defend yourself against an assailant, you will need strength, flexibility, stamina, and stability. Fostering these traits will sculpt and tone your body.

This type of class will also leave you feeling empowered. This can be especially helpful if you have been victimized in the past. Coping with this type of distress can disrupt your experience of safety. With time and practice, you will obtain that empowerment and a greater sense of self-worth.

True friendships can also be forged with people attending the same class. Chances are, you will have a few things in common with your classmates since most of you have similar goals. This can be especially beneficial if you are new to the area or have trouble making friends spontaneously. Developing closer connections with people whole live nearby can improve your sense of confidence and security. You will feel safer in your community and anywhere you choose to travel.

Naturally, safety is the biggest benefit of taking a self-defense class. You will develop a greater awareness of your movements and surroundings. This will allow you to predict and evade harmful situations before they even happen – which is the ultimate goal.

You will also learn how to react to dangerous scenarios that cannot be avoided. Hands-on practice will help you prepare and develop skills for fighting off an assailant. While many of us go through life never expecting to require this type of training, it will become priceless should find yourself under attack.

After all, according to the statistics, people do get violently attacked every day. Training in self-defense tactics will allow you to assess the safety of a location or situation and avoid those with the potential for danger. It will also help you defend yourself in situations that are unavoidable. After taking a self-defense class, you will know how to protect yourself and the people you love.

A good self-defense class will be geared towards teaching you how to escape a dangerous situation as quickly as possible in the first instance and counter attacking in the second.

This training might keep you from being assaulted or raped. It can also save your life. No tuition fee or time commitment should seem too large when looked at from this perspective. Your safety is certainly worth more.

There is a wide selection of self-defense classes available. Many of these classes are tied to a particular Martial Art, while others use certain aspects of multiple styles. So which is for you?...

Which Self-Defense or Martial Arts Class Should I Choose?

Not all self-defense classes or instructors are created equal. You will want to weigh all of your options to determine which class offers the best quality at the right price. You will be committing your time, energy, and money, so you deserve a sound return on your investment.

A little research can help you find a class that will provide both the confidence and the skills needed to defend yourself against a physical threat.

In addition to being effective, a good self-defense or Martial Arts class will also be enjoyable. You should find yourself excited to attend and open to participating. After all, if you don't enjoy it, you won't attend and hence will not receive any of the benefits.

Below you will find a list which details the many ways to identify whether a particular class will develop the skills and confidence you desire:

1. **Consider Your Skill Level:** Honestly assess your own fitness and experience levels. The class you choose should match your ability. While a challenging class may look more enticing, you should start with the basics to avoid feeling overwhelmed.

2. **Listen for Recommendations:** The best way to determine whether a class is worth your time is to get an honest review from a friend or neighbor who has participated in the class you are considering.

3. **Contact the Police Department:** Most police stations will have a listing of approved self-defense classes in your area. The list should include licensed courses with instructors of good repute.

4. **Meet With the Teacher:** Talking with the instructor will help you learn more about their teaching style and personality. Your instructor should focus more on avoiding bad situations than engaging in conflict. The importance of a good coach cannot be overstated.

5. **Shadow a Class:** Ask to sit it on a class. Pay attention to how easily the students seem to understand what the teacher is trying to convey. By the end of the class, you should be able to determine if you feel comfortable with the instructor and potential classmates.

6. **Enjoy the Process:** While self-defense is a serious subject, classes do not have to be boring or tedious. A good

instructor will add enough entertainment to keep each lesson interesting. You will not be motivated to return if you do not enjoy each session. Seek an instructor who knows how to make learning a fun process.

7. **Addressing the Potential for Panic:** While you will need physical skills to fend off an attacker, your emotional state can play an ever bigger part in the outcome. A good self-defense class will help you prepare for the stress of a dangerous situation. You will need to learn to stay calm and focus on your training. Reducing the effects of fear and panic should be included in the lesson plan.

Before you begin your search, sit down and decide what you expect to gain. You may prefer a laid back class if your goal is to make friends and have a good time. Or you may prefer a more technical and serious class if you are ready to get down to business and learn some advanced techniques.

Every self-defense class will teach skills that can be used to escape danger, but not every class will be the right match for your personality and expectations. The right class will improve your confidence and provide quality self-defense training.

Recommendations:

The following are some broad recommendations depending on your requirements. Note that the individual classes and the manner in which they are taught make a great difference, so it's always worth investigating your local club before making a choice.

Bear in mind that traditional Martial Arts have many great benefits but are quite limited in their modern self-defense applications. If looking after yourself is your main goal, "pure" self-defense styles will work best for you.

Reality-based/Modern/Pure Self Defense:

- Krav Maga
- Systema
- Keysi Fighting Method/Defense Lab
- Defendo
- Military based combat

Ground Fighting, Grappling, and Wrestling styles:

- Sambo
- Brazilian JuJitsu
- Wrestling
- Judo

Traditional Striking Arts:

- Karate
- Kung Fu
- Tae kwon do
- Kickboxing
- Muay Thai
- Boxing
- Silat

Cross Training:
- Vale Tudo
- MMA (Mixed Martial Arts)

Weapon Based:

- Eskrima
- Kendo
- Modern stick fighting

How to Hack Your Brain, Defend Your Body

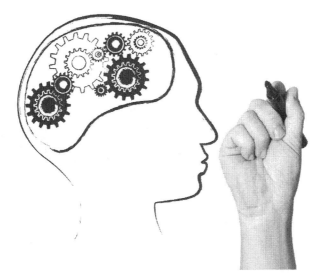

One of the most interesting facets of self-defense is that 90% of the battle is over before any fists are even thrown. Preparation is of course key, but your psychological state also plays a huge role and makes the difference between handling a situation quickly and calmly or being flustered and skittish – triggering potential danger.

Stress will always trigger unwanted bodily reactions, but with the right knowledge, you can learn a few simple tricks to control your physical being via your mind and ensure you stay in control of your actions should the worst happen.

Rather than entering some zen-like meditative state on a mountaintop, we are aiming to be fully aware of the danger in front of us, without letting it control our mind. Our goal is to be alert but relaxed. Our hands are up and ready to protect our bodies, but the mind is focused and unhurried.

The nature of violence will always threaten to overwhelm our senses, so never feel bad for experiencing panic. However, if you can use even one of the following methods and reduce panic by only 10%, you will be better prepared than most.

1. Breathe

It sounds obvious; after all we all know how to breathe, but keeping your breathing steady and controlled is a major help in maintaining a calm, focused mind.

A simple way to regulate this is to count the inhalation and exhalation.

- Breathe in for a count of 4
- Hold for a count of 4
- Breathe out for a count of 4
- Repeat

This is a technique borrowed from meditation and is often known as Mindful Breathing. By bringing our attention to our inhalations and exhalations, we not only calm the body but also reduce distractions of the mind.

And while we are on the topic…

2. Mindfulness

Mindfulness is another excellent method borrowed from meditation. Put simply, it is a method of becoming aware of your physical body without judgment or over-thinking.

This last part is particularly useful when we start to panic and the heart starts racing:

- Bring your attention to how you physically feel
- Are you hot, cold, tense, or relaxed?
- Do not judge the sensations – just let them be there
- Do not worry about what has happened or what might happen
- Just focus on the here and now, and your place in it

(See 'Learn From Nature' for more details)

Deflection

When a scary or stressful situation occurs, our minds get completely stuck in the second-by-second event, which only serves to further stress us out. We center on minute details which spins the stress faster and faster in our mind until we can't handle it.

One simple tip to combat this is to briefly bring your thoughts to something you enjoy that you know you will do after the event, i.e. what you will do tomorrow, a friend you will see, or great meal you will have.

It can also work for enjoyable events that have already happened. The more stimulating and memorable the event, the more it will draw you away from stress and towards simple alertness.

Think about that time at the beach, the crazy night out you once had, or that girl/guy you once hooked up with. Whatever works as a fond and powerful memory for you!

Gradual Acceptance

There is an old saying that if you throw a frog into hot water, it will instantly jump out, but if you throw a frog in cold water and gradually heat it, the frog will happily stay and cook alive.

I'm not sure who came up with that idea, and I'd advise passing on any dinner invites, but the principal is that we find it much easier to accept things in life if they are gradual, rather than big changes.

In a self-defense situation, you can use this yourself. Of course, many encounters are quick and allow no time for speaking with an opponent, but in the unfortunate scenario of being trapped in an extended threat scenario or an individual asking for a "fight", you can use "gradual acceptance" to give yourself a better chance or escape altogether.

Start small with something they will easily agree to. If this works out in your favor, then try something else. You don't even need to ask them per se. Just take little, easy steps toward your goal.

> *"Let me just take off my jacket."*
> *"I just need to put my phone down."*
> *"Please can I keep this on?"*
> *"You can put the weapon down, it's not needed."*
> *"Let's not do this here."*
> *"You should just let me go, it's much easier."*

There are many different options that you can adapt for your own use. Each step should gradually build on the last. By gently, and gradually tipping a situation in your favor, you can sway the mind of an attacker and possibly avoid conflict altogether.

NOTE: This technique is really only suited for extended threats with time to defuse the situation. If the danger is immediate and quick, your reaction should be the same.

Here are a few further mantras to consider...

Learn from Nature

Welcome to the Jungle

This isn't some motivational "eye of the tiger" pep talk chapter but a consideration for ensuring survival. As humans we are quite unique in that we have the most developed brains on earth, and yet in so many ways this works against us.

In situations where we need that primal fight or flight instinct, our minds become clouded with a thousand thoughts at once.

What would my friends say?
Do I look like an idiot if I say this?
Is this illegal?
What if I kill him?
What if he kills me?

Yet look to the animal kingdom, and there are no hesitations in nature. When two wild creatures get aggressive, they fight hard and/or they leave. They don't wonder how it looks, they don't consider the future. They just fight tooth and nail and/or run. They do it because that is the way to survive in the wild. On the rare occasion violence threatens you, it's time to realize you have briefly left civilization and entered the wild.

Of course a physical response should always be carefully considered, but once you decide to act, try to think like an animal. Fight dirty, fight hard, and fight like your life depends on it, because it might!

When things kick off, try to use "Mindfulness" to bring your awareness to the present. Mindfulness is a powerful technique used for thousands of years in meditation but also for psychotherapy stress relief and even sports.

The basic principle is simple:

- Do not focus on what might or could happen
- Do not focus on what has happened
- Bring your attention to the very moment you are in
- Become aware of all your sensations without judging them

The safeguard, of course, to prevent over-injuring someone is to realize that once you have incapacitated, injured, or distracted your attacker; it is time for you to make your escape. No hanging around, no thinking, just run.

Panic Won't Help. Let it go.

It's easy to say "don't panic", but it is a harsh truth that you will almost certainly panic at the start of a violent situation. We just aren't built to deal with them in our daily lives, and the stress response is our body's way of handling this. Understand that stress is actually necessary for us to survive. It is a natural bodily instinct, and once you start to see it that way, some of the sting is taken out.

You can train yourself to prepare for stress to a degree, but how you handle the rest of an encounter can steer your success. To ensure we aren't ruled by adrenaline should the worst happen, we need to break it down to a simple truth.

Consider this:

Whether you panic or not, it's still happening.

That's it.

Yes, this is happening; yes, it's scary; and yes, you are aware of it, but panicking will not change that, so let it go.

Bring your attention to a calm place and focus on breathing. Don't worry about what has happened, will happen, or might happen.

Forget over-thinking, and be decisive. Avoid the threat, counter attack if needed, and escape. Keep it simple.

Don't Let Pride Win.

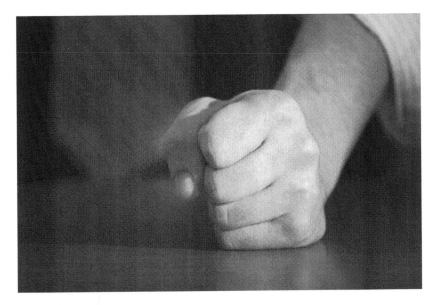

Pride will make you do both great and stupid things in life, but in Self-Defense, pride can become your worst enemy. Men are especially susceptible to this particular deadly sin but macho posturing can affect all of us.

We are naturally proud of the things we have achieved in life and our family and friends around us. But when someone threatens that pride, you have to make a choice on how to respond. Of course, a physical threat should always be handled quickly and with appropriate force, but a verbal or social threat can be the precursor to further danger. How you handle a loud-mouth can make a big difference.

Alcohol is a major source of violent crime, and many of these incidents start with a passing remark or glance that escalates. While it's impossible to control how others act, you can control how you respond.

If you wish to master verbal self-defense, consider becoming Teflon; *everything slides off you.*

By maintaining control and not letting emotion take over, you are becoming the better man or woman – even if it might be hard to see at the time. However, if you resort to violence over a few words, you are lowering yourself to their level.

That isn't to say you should become a meek, retiring wallflower if you aren't normally. What it means is that you should be your normal self, and never get goaded into unnecessary aggression, whatever the opponent says.

So how do you know whether to respond or not?

The Ten Year Rule

One way to make a positive choice in either engaging or ignoring an opponent is to use the "10 Year Rule".

Simply put, each time you feel anger taking over or find yourself offended by someone, take a breath and consider how the 'future you' would feel about this in 10 years' time.

- *In 10 years' time, would it really matter what some drunken idiot said on a random night out?*

Probably not.

- *In 10 years' time, would you really care about some guy that was eying your partner for a couple of minutes?*

You wouldn't even remember the incident.

- *In 10 years' time, would you remember the individual who went for you with a knife?*

Definitely. It's time to act.

The only case where you should make a move is when you are fearful for your life, not fearful for your reputation. In 10 years' time, you won't remember any insults or verbal threats thrown around one evening on the town, but in 10 years' time, you would remember a knife wound or broken nose.

Always try to get perspective on your actions and consider how 'future you' would view your actions.

How to Spot a Threat Before it Happens

When violence is imminent, you start to panic, breathing speeds up, and your pulse quickens, but it's not just the heart rate of the victim that will rise. Attackers too will experience a change in their body as they prepare themselves for what's to come.

If you can learn the signs of impending danger, you can learn to avoid them. If someone starts to look aggressive, they are best avoided. If this is not possible, they are best placated. If both these have failed, and only if both have failed, it's time to consider your position, potential counter attacking, and escape.

Of course, everyone is different. Some people are strung out on drugs or alcohol, so they may exhibit none of these signs, though hopefully they will show far more obvious ones. Other people still have psychological issues and may appear calm and collected, but rather than worry about the outside chances of cold, calculating nut-jobs, we always focus on the most likely scenario. In this case, the typical mugger or average Joe looking for a fight will exhibit one or several of the following:

- *Change of voice pitch/speed*

A common trait of stress is the change in pitch or speed of a person's voice. As emotions start to take hold, it becomes increasingly difficult to focus on calm, reasoned conversation. If you observe someone approaching you and their voice keeps breaking or they speed up and slow down the way they talk, it can be a sign that you need to be wary.

- *Repetition*

Commonly seen among drunks trying to enter a bar or club, repetition occurs because an individual is losing control of the situation. As adrenaline starts to cloud their thoughts, the only goal they can see is the most obvious one, and this is reflected in their speech pattern.

If an agitated individual keeps insisting on something or seems to continually refer to the same point, be aware of a potentially impending threat.

- *Flushed face*

Fairly obvious, this one. When we get stressed, our blood flow increases. If an attacker is preparing for violence, the adrenaline will stimulate an increased heart rate and dilation of the blood vessels to prepare the body for action. This can easily be spotted in a red or flushed complexion on the face.

The same is true of people who have just been exercising, however. So don't assume everyone coming out of the gym is about to mug you! Just be aware that increased redness *can* signal a response to stress.

- *Being nice for no reason.*

Sometimes it pays to be cynical. If a friend or neighbor offers to help you with your shopping, that's fine. But if a random stranger approaches you in a parking lot and offers the same, it's time to firmly but politely say, "No thanks".

Some aggressors use 'being nice' as a way to initially lower the defenses of a target. Once you agree to the help, they have a window into your car, apartment, or life.

- **Over Sharing**

If someone approaches you asking for the time or some change for a bus, it may be innocent. But if they follow this up with lots of unnecessary details of why they need it, there could be cause for concern.

Over sharing pointless details is a classic sign of deception. When we lie about something, we often over-compensate by telling others about excessive specifics.

"I need some change, because the bus will be here soon, and I have to meet my girlfriend and her brother in 20 minutes over by the park before we go to..." etc. etc.

"Do you have the time? I'm guessing it's about 3:30pm, but I left my watch at home, and I'd normally use my phone, but it broke last week when I was at the..." etc. etc.

Of course they could just be lying to cover up some embarrassment or personal issue, but it pays to be aware of the deception.

What Can I Do?

The last thing you want to do in a dangerous situation is start using the same signals as the threat. This just escalates the encounter as both parties get more and more stressed.

The simplest way to avoid making a scenario worse if you come across anyone exhibiting any of these signs is to do the opposite. In most cases, this will serve to calm a person down and placate the danger.

If they are speaking fast, looking flushed and stressed, you respond by being calm and assertive.

If they seem to be approaching you for unwarranted help and talking a lot, you become laconic and offer a succinct and short reply to the negative, while moving the other way. (Though never losing sight of them)

In each case, we try to initially cancel out the rising stress of the situation and take control of what is happening.

Why You Should Always 'Control Your Space'

An important philosophy of self-protection is that of personal space. That is the area directly around you within arm or leg distance. You can check it right now by holding out your arms and spinning around. If you imagine the circular shape this creates, this is your zone and you should be safe within it.

This shape also flows behind you. Many people forget this but a threat from behind is just as dangerous, or perhaps even more so than the one in front.

Controlling this space is absolutely crucial for staying safe on the streets. Friends and family may enter it, but strangers do not unless you trust them. The open-palm guard, as shown in this book and my first, is an effective barrier for any would-be close-encounters. With palms facing an individual, they have to make a concerted effort to enter your space.

If they do this, it is clear they mean to get close, and their movements are no accident.

The Shove

In some cases, you can clear this space around you without initiating violence by a good hard shove. This is an especially powerful technique for women against overly amorous drunk guys who stumble out of bars and clubs looking for a "hug".

Both palms pushed hard and fast against a man's chest will not cause any long term damage but will push him back and can knock the breath from him.

Importantly, don't gently push against him gradually using more and more strength – which will eventually fail. This gives him time to resist and lean in. Instead, get the hands in place and give a short sharp shove back with everything you have straight away.

Gentlemen: This method is also effective for getting other guys away from you, but be careful; using the chest shove against women can be construed as sexual assault. Try pushing them away firmly by their shoulders instead.

The rules:

- You have a right to your personal space.
- No one enters your space without you allowing it.
- If they do enter, you respond hard and fast.
- Clear your space as fast as possible, and ensure they cannot re-enter.

How to Never Get Hit... (Using 'The Triangle')

If you ever see skilled martial artists or boxers, you will notice they do not move in a linear fashion but use their feet to make it hard for an opponent to land a strike. The street isn't a competition, so the movement is slightly different, but the concept is the same.

The simplest way to ensure you don't go down in any attack is to ensure you don't get hit. Sure, you can try to block and counter an incoming attack using various techniques, but the single most effective method is to make it impossible for an aggressor to land a hit on you in the first place.

There are many stances and clever footwork drills on offer to remove you from danger, but unfortunately when a stressful situation develops, it can become easy to forget your positioning and present an easy target.

"Triangle movement", however, is a dead-simple principle ensuring you remain out of range of any attacker and gives you the opportunity to counter-strike if needed.

If someone is going to hit you, regardless of technique, they need two things:

- **To cover the distance from their arm or leg to your body**
- **To hit the center of the target on your body to do the damage**

Distance + Accuracy = Successful Strike

Take away either of these, and you drastically reduce the odds of being struck because the equation falls apart.

If an attacker is exactly on target but too far away, they cannot land a strike.

If an attacker is close enough but misses the target, they cannot land a strike.

So how can we make this principle even more powerful? By taking away both the distance **AND** targeting. "Triangle movement" uses the idea that an attacker can usually only strike within a certain arc and at a certain distance. Beyond this, they cannot affect you in any way (beyond verbal threats).

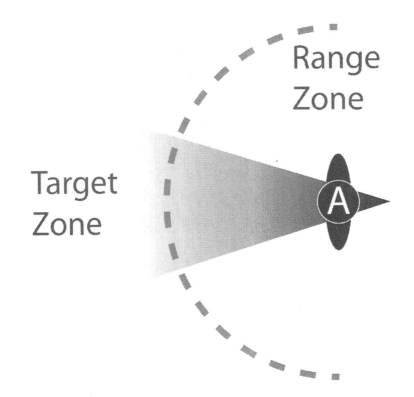

In the above diagram, 'A' represents the attacker and the dashed line shows how far an attacker could potentially reach. The gray area meanwhile demonstrates the area of threat or the parts an aggressor would most likely target.

If you were thinking there is one very bad place to be in that diagram, you were right...

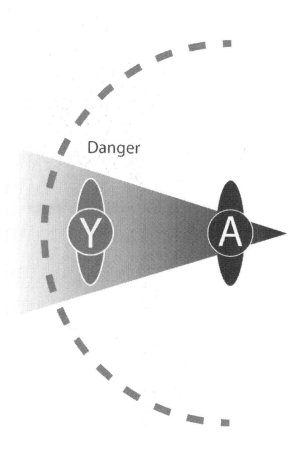

Danger

Here of course, 'Y' represents you, and we can clearly see the most dangerous area to be in, which is within both the range **and** target zone of an attacker who could pivot around. (Attackers don't usually stand still!)

Conversely there is an ultimate safe zone to be in, and this is where we aim to place ourselves in a self-defense scenario.

Safe Zone (You)

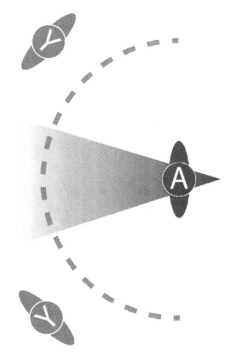

Safe Zone (You)

Now we see that in either of the "safe" positions, it is impossible for the attacker to inflict any damage, as 'Y' is both out of the target zone **and** beyond reach. Of course, you cannot inflict any damage yourself, but if you wish to avoid injury, which is the no.1 goal, these points are the places to be.

Note also that the shapes now form a Triangle. If you can maintain this triangle of both distance and targeting with the attacker, it will not matter where he/she moves as you will be out of danger.

To keep this safe area, you must match an opponent's movement. They go forward, you go back; they go left, you go right.

Martial Artists and combat arts practitioners are naturally quite talented at this because sparring requires similar skills in distance and timing, but anyone can practice it with a fun exercise:

Distance and Target Exercise

-   Grab a friend or partner. One of you tucks a small colored cloth or marker flag into your collar with the end hanging out. (Waistband can also be used for variation.)

-   Start by facing each other, and set a stopwatch for 30 seconds.

-   On "go', the aim of the 'attacker' is to snatch the colored cloth, while the aim of the 'defender' is to protect it for the duration.

-   Once one person has 'won' or the time expires, swap over and repeat until both have tried the exercise a few times.

This fun little drill simulates the effect of moving with an opponent and staying out of range and target. You will find it is quite exhausting though, which is why we always promote an avoidance, counter, and escape approach in Self-defense. Fighting is just too tiring!

Pre-Emptive Striking (And Should I Do It?)

For those unfamiliar with the term, a pre-emptive strike is essentially making the first move in anticipation of an enemy threat, with the aim of neutralizing that danger before it fully takes form.

It is a concept hotly debated among Martial Artists and self-defense coaches.

On one hand, striking first and being active before your opponent gives you a great advantage both physically and psychologically, while potentially catching an aggressor off guard and deterring any opportunists from violence before it happens. You are also taking control of the scenario and directing it in the way you desire.

Many people will be simply put off by an aggressive individual, and you will no-longer be perceived as a victim.

On the other hand however, making the first move changes the scenario from one of self-defense to that of a fight. You are suddenly the attacker, and no matter how good your intentions are, to any passerby it may seem as if you started the altercation.

So how do you know whether to hit first?

I like to think of pre-emptive striking as only viable after a number of things have occurred. In this sense, it is not pre-emptive at all (other than in name), but a considered and reasonable response to a number of events.

The following list details events that must occur for you to consider attacking first. If they don't, then you are at a legal and moral risk of becoming the attacker.

Your Checklist:

- **You fear for your life and/or safety**
- **You have no reasonable means of escape**
- **You have no other choice**
- **You fully believe an attack against you is imminent**

If all these criteria are met and you do respond in advance of imminent danger, you will have a much stronger position legally than if you just hit someone because of a "bad feeling". Not to mention that you won't have escalated a situation unless there was no other recourse.

It should be noted that if you do decide to strike, you should do so hard and fast. Commit fully, but also stop fully once a threat has been neutralized. The force used, as always, should also be proportionate to the threat faced.

For more understanding, (and a fascinating History lesson), search for 'The Caroline Test' regarding pre-emptive self-defense.

How to Use Everyday Objects as Weapons

One of the most enduring self-defense myths involves the use of everyday objects to protect yourself should the worst happen. This is great in principle and can work in some cases, but a quick scan of the internet reveals lots of tips written by people who have clearly never been in a violent position.

"Spray a perfume bottle in an attacker's eyes."

Or

"Put a key between your fingers for an improvised brass knuckle."

I'm not suggesting these techniques don't work; they do. It's just that the realistic application of each takes far longer than would be practical on the street. We simply don't have the time or thought process in place when it all kicks off to perform any complicated techniques.

Would you really want to be fishing around in your bag to find a bottle of perfume or deodorant while someone is attacking you?

Do you think you will have the time or co-ordination to place a key between your knuckles (which will likely just fall out or likely do you more damage than them)?

If you do have time to prepare these things, then I have bad news. It's not self-defense, it's a fight. The majority of street situations are brutal, fast, and unplanned leaving no time for this kind of pre-meditation.

The only case they may have some validity in would be an extended sexual assault, but even then you are likely to be better off relying on elbows and fingers than fashioning some rudimentary weapons.

Remember a violent encounter will usually be:

Fast

Unexpected
Confusing

So what can I use?

There are, however, a few items most people carry that can be used in defense at the last minute without any thinking. These are simple, uncomplicated methods you can employ to give you valuable escape time (not fighting time).

Coins

Many of us carry a pocketful of coins around as change for vending machines, parking meters, or just leftover from recent purchases. It may be annoying in your pocket but can serve as a great distraction in a tight spot.

- If a situation is escalating, grab a handful of coins and throw them hard and fast at your opponent's eyes.

- If you are lucky, you may hit and temporarily blind them, but even if you don't, they will instinctively raise their hands to protect the face

- Once their arms are up, kick hard to the groin or strike with your palm to their chest

- Escape the scene; run.

Keys

Most people carry keys, and they can be used effectively, but trying to place them carefully between your fingers or creating some kind of brass knuckle effect as many places suggest is just unrealistic. Instead, consider how you would use them if you were fighting for your life.

- Once violence is inevitable, quickly grab your keys firmly in one hand with bits sticking out all over – don't worry about it being even as long as it isn't sticking into your own palm. Preferably, hook one finger through a keyring and hold the keys outside your knuckle.

- Whip the keys up, and lash them across the attackers face roughly. (Think of the way an animal would claw.)

- If you had the finger through the keyring, you can also strike in a punch style.

- If you were unable to hook them, simple flay them across the attackers face and make for your escape. Do not worry about holding onto them.

Your Jacket

If you are wearing a long coat or thick jacket, it can become a hindrance if you need to move quickly. It might look fashionable but if you know that knee-length number is heavy and tight it can be best to remove it.

- If violence is imminent remove the heavy jacket in advance

(If it is actually underway do not waste time trying to take a coat off however)

- In the case of being threatened by a knife you can quickly throw the jacket at the attackers arm and knife hand – restricting their movement momentarily and briefly protecting yourself from any wild slashes.

- Use the distraction to escape

One exception may be leather jackets. Genuine leather does offer significant protection, which is why motorcyclists prefer them so much, and so they can be left on provided you can still move freely.

The Power of the Humble Flashlight

The humble flashlight is one of the most overlooked tools in self-defense, mostly due to the fact that people see it for its utility use, rather than self-protection. For this very reason, they are particularly effective as "stealth" weapons, completely legal to carry, unassuming, and powerful in a number of ways.

Of course, the obvious application of a flashlight or "torch" if you are European, is for illuminating dark areas, which could be essential if you find yourself in a dim parking lot or a power cut, but the same light can also be used to distract an attacker.

In a dark environment, our pupils dilate to let more light in; this is how we adjust to the change in light. However, this adjustment takes several seconds to a few minutes depending on the change. If you suddenly flash a bright light in the face of a potential threat, you will force their eyes to adjust, temporarily blinding them.

This period of disorientation is used effectively worldwide by military and police forces. *Ever wondered why Police so often carry a huge flashlight?*

Using your flashlight as a self-defense tool:

- Ensure you have a well-made, bright, and easily portable flash light. (Not one that only works half the time.) Waterproof is also recommended.

- Ensure it is 'click-on' (i.e. a button turns it on and off.) "Twist-on" works too but is not as instant and requires two hands.

- Use good quality batteries, and check them every couple of months. Lithium batteries are generally recommended (if your flashlight can take them). These batteries usually last many more years than alkaline, offer a brighter beam, and are less likely to leak.

- Don't wave the flashlight around at an attacker. If you use it, just switch the beam on once and quickly aim directly at their eyes.

- They will usually shield their face and have trouble seeing. Use this period to escape the danger and leave for better lit areas.

The added secret:

Perhaps the most overlooked aspect of a flashlight is that it is a blunt force weapon in itself. Yes, the beam is useful as a distraction, but the body of a torch is a great weapon also.

- Small palm-held flashlights work just like a Kubotan (see later) and are effective for hammer-fist strikes and sharp jabs to the throat and soft tissue.

- Large multi-cell flashlights are of course great for striking like a bat or bar, but they also work as a significant visual deterrent – the very reason why so many security guards, who cannot carry 'weapons', carry these. They look intimidating.

How to Choose Self-Defense "Weapons"

Keychain Weapons

Many self-defense weapons are available for purchase, ranging from the innocuous to the dangerous.

Keychain devices are becoming increasingly popular as a subtle form of carried weapon. Some self-defense key chains are inconspicuously made to look like animals or lengths of wood or plastic.

Kubotan

The Kubotan is essentially just a lump of wood and herein lies its strength. As a hard length of little more size than a marker pen, the Kubotan is subtle, unlikely (not impossible) to cause legal ramifications through carrying, and effective if used correctly.

Originally conceived in the late Seventies by a famed Karate master working with Police departments at the time, it is considered one of the most understated close-quarter defense weapons.

Usually about 15 centimeters, or six inches, long and 1.25 centimeters, or ½ inch thick. This solid baton can also be used as a keychain so that it is always with you.

How are they used?

There are entire books on the potential applications of the Kubotan, but the simplest and most effective methods are one of three techniques:

1. Used as part of a keychain. Grasp the Kubotan as a handle, and turn your keys into a flail of sorts. Swing for an attacker's face

and eyes.

2. Hold the Kubotan like a baton with the end sticking out of the base of your fist. Using hammer fist motions (see later), jab for the eyes or, most effectively, the throat.

3. Again hold the Kubotan like a baton, but this time utilize the upper part above your fist, stabilized by a thumb. (Think how wizards would use a wand). Again, jab for soft tissue.

For the greatest impact, focus your Kubotan towards the more sensitive parts of your assailant such as their forearm, knuckles, shin, nose, spine, temple, ribs, solar plexus, groin, eyes, or neck. It can be used with a forceful, stabbing motion, or pushed firmly against pressure points.

If you do not have a Kubotan handy, you can improvise with nearby objects presenting similar characteristics. A pen, flashlight, dowel, electronic cigarette, or hairbrush may well do the trick. Special metal pens are sometimes also sold as defense weapons and can be used in the same manner as a Kubotan.

An often neglected aspect of self-defense is knowing your rights. Kubotans generally exist in either the legal or gray areas of the law. As a round lump of wood or keyring, they are fairly inoffensive, but once you start opting for the sharpened or metal versions, there can be some risk.

At the time of writing this there are little to no restrictions to carrying a Kubotan in the United States. The spiked version however is considered an offensive-weapon according to the British crime-prevention website. The legality of carrying a non-spiked version in the UK is open to interpretation in the eyes of a court.

Mace or Pepper Spray

While used in a similar manner and often confused within the media, pepper spray and mace are not actually the same thing. Like keychain weapons, they are often carried for self-defense.

True mace is actually a neurotoxin. It can make your opponent feel as though their skin and eyes are burning intensely. This is due to membrane irritation. The effects should take place within five to thirty seconds after application. However, some people seem to be immune to the effects, particularly those who are intoxicated or under the influence of narcotics.

It is important not to confuse true mace with the popular *Mace* brand. Today the manufacturer *Mace* produces a variety of self-defense sprays including both true mace and pepper spray blends. You should read all packaging and product descriptions carefully to know what you are purchasing.

Pepper spray on the other hand uses concentrated compounds from hot peppers – hence the name. It is not an irritant like mace per se. It is an inflammatory agent and considered superior in some cases since it will cause discomfort and pain to anyone it contacts.

The effects should happen almost instantly and it can be temporarily blinding if sprayed in your attacker's eyes. If possible you might want to opt for one that is labeled "police grade". Some manufactures dilute the chemicals to make a greater profit. The police grade formulas generally prove to be both potent and effective.

You can purchase both mace and pepper spray in small canisters which can be attached to your key-ring, or kept in discreet locations.

- *It may sound obvious, but never use Mace or Pepper Spray while running or in strong winds. The last thing you want is to be hit by your own spray!*

Again, the legality of carrying these items varies around the world. In the USA, they are generally accepted as a self-defense item, whereas in the UK, they are illegal and classified as "offensive weapons". Always check your local laws.

Should I Carry a Firearm or Knife?

This is a debate that has raged for many years across many countries. Firstly, I would always advise remaining within the law. If firearms are illegal for personal carry in your country, don't be tempted to carry one just in case. There are plenty of effective alternatives, and if you get caught with one when you aren't supposed to have it, you can expect a stint in prison.

Ultimately, the choice of weapon carrying is a personal one. I prefer to focus on the usage of improvised everyday items or pure "defense-only" items as weapons rather than the use of actual purpose made tools like firearms, or god forbid, knives. (Fun fact: carry a knife for self-defense and chances are *you* will get stabbed with it.)

To my mind, guns and blades require a level of pre-meditation that changes the scenario from one of self-protection to one of combat. If you have time to draw and fire a weapon, you have time to run away.

It's also worth bearing in mind that in many parts of Europe and the UK, use and even ownership of such weapons is illegal in itself, though the laws in the USA are more relaxed in many states.

I realize this isn't always the case of course; it's impossible to plan for every scenario, and these are just my personal views. I prefer to focus on the unexpected close-range type assaults that are more common. If you are looking for guides on using concealed carry weapons or edged weapons there are many excellent books and training schools for these subjects.

How to Pick Targets on Your Opponent

Whichever way you look at it, the human body is essentially a big bag of organs held together by a few bones. On the outside, we have a tough layer of skin and muscle keeping it all together, but at several special points, these organs and bones are closest to the surface and present a unique chance for a defender to get the upper hand over an attacker.

The amazing thing about these points is that no matter how big, tough, or strong the opponent, the weaknesses are the same. It's just not possible to toughen up some parts of the body regardless of how long you spend in training or down the gym.

I covered many specific strikes and counter attacks in the first book, but here we will look at specific targets and the best way to use them to your advantage.

There are of course many other targets and you should feel free to exploit anything you can. The following are simply the most obvious and easily accessible targets on an opponent.

1. Eyes

It's not just humans that have a weak point at the eyes. Pretty much every creature has the same weakness. Experts suggest that if you are attacked by a dog, alligator, or heck, even a shark, it is recommended you go for the eyes.

Humans are the same. We simply don't have any skin or muscle covering our eyes, and the eyelids are only there to prevent dust and debris from entering, not any force.

If you can blind someone temporarily, you stand an excellent chance of escaping since eyesight is the sense we rely on most.

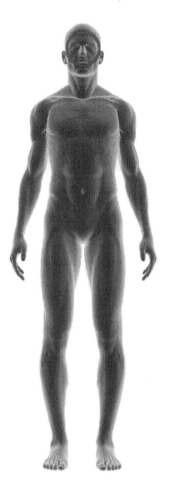

Consider:

- Pokes and finger jabs
- Raking fingers across the face
- Thrown dust, dirt, sand, or other fine powder
- Mace and pepper spray; designed specifically for this purpose
- Nose strike (Getting hit in the nose causes an automatic reaction of watery eyes.)

2. Throat

The throat is one of the most overlooked target zones for some reason. Perhaps because it is not a 'traditional' fighting target as seen in movies and TV, and the face presents a more obvious place to focus attacks on. Despite this, the throat is actually a perfect spot to aim for in self-defense due to its vulnerability and location.

Although there are muscles around the neck like the SCM (sternocleidomastoid), it is near impossible to build these up adequately and the entire region is mostly soft tissue perfect for a strike no matter how big or strong an opponent is.

The main benefit of targeting this area is of course the windpipe or Trachea. A sharp jab or punch to the throat can temporarily (or permanently) collapse the air flow to an attacker's body. This not only leaves them gasping for breath but creates an instant psychological block on their movements.

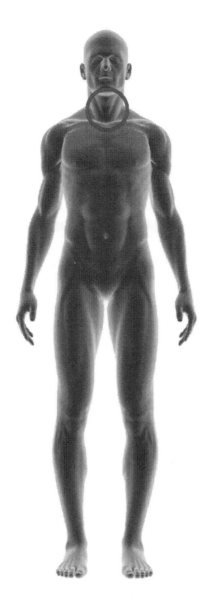

Consider:

- Throat jam (See later)
- Punch or jab
- Constriction or choke (Not recommended for a quick escape)

3. Solar Plexus

The Solar Plexus has several names but is most commonly also called the Sternum. Essentially, the Plexus or 'Nexus' element refers to the nerve cluster in the area at the center of the chest where the ribs meet.

This is an excellent target for numerous strikes, not only because of the impact on an attacker's nervous system but for the ease with which you can incapacitate someone without causing long-term damage.

A sharp palm-strike to this spot can break ribs, but more often than not it 'winds' an opponent causing them to collapse or struggle in getting their breath – perfect if you are trying to escape.

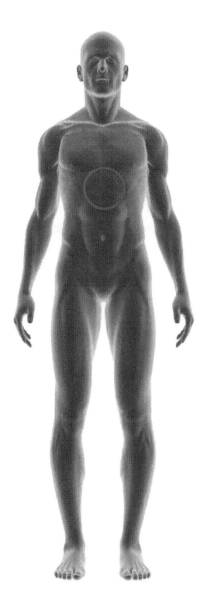

Consider:

- Palm Strike
- Punch

4. Groin

The groin is a popular target in many self-defense techniques because of its sensitivity – especially for men. An effective groin strike can be utterly devastating, but also bear in mind that it typically requires a closer range to be effective, and the subsequent doubling-up of an opponent can cause problems if you aren't aware of it.

If you prefer to maintain distance, which is recommended, consider a groin kick rather than knee strike to the area. Strikes here can also be easily deflected by simply turning to the side, so if you decide to employ one you either need to make it very quick or lead with a high technique like a hammer-fist to distract the opponent first.

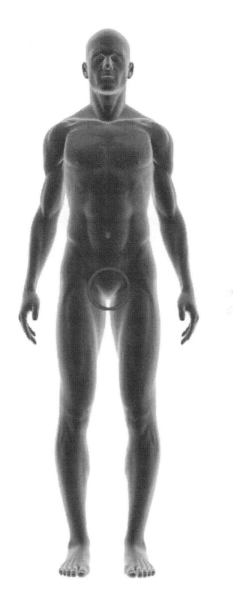

Consider:

- Front kick
- Knee strike

5. Kneecap

The kneecap (or Patella) is another oft-overlooked target, and yet it forms a vital connection through the stabilization of the whole body. The knee is, of course, designed to bend in one direction, so any sharp application of power against another direction, either backwards or to the side, can quickly remove an opponent's ability to fight or chase.

Snap kicks and low, side-kicks are most effective for this region.

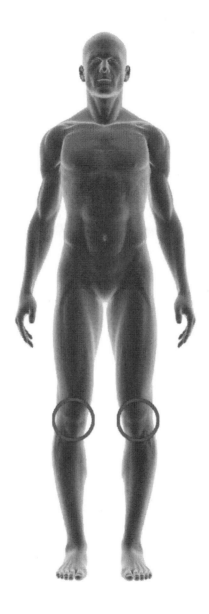

Consider:

- Side kick – to side of knee
- Snap kick striking with the hard toe part of the shoe
- Front Kick or stomp to the front of the kneecap

6. Shins

While the shins are relatively strong bones, they are also a very sensitive area on most people, and because they are low and easily accessible, they offer a convenient target for inflicting pain as a distraction or to reduce mobility against an attacker.

Due to the shape of the Shin Bone (or Tibia), twisting the foot slightly and creating a wider striking zone can work better in hitting the target.

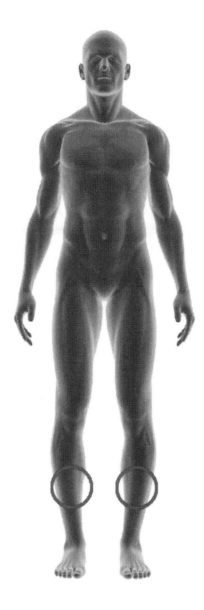

Consider:

- Side kick – at a downward angle
- Scraping kick – scraping the instep of your foot downwards
- Snap kick – using the hard toe portion of the shoe

Do Pressure Points Really Work

If you believe action movies, then you'd be forgiven for thinking
a single deadly touch in the right place might be able to instantly
incapacitate someone no matter how big and scary they are. Of
course, the knowledge of this touch of death is usually only
taught by the most mysterious and wizened of Martial Arts
masters.

Luckily, the truth is a little more accessible. Far from being some
mythical secret, pressure points are really just extra sensitive parts of
the body where either clusters of nerves pass through making the area
more receptive to pain, or organs close to the surface are more
vulnerable since they are away from the usual skeletal or muscular
protection.

Consider Pressure Points as a bonus. They are unlikely to win a fight on their own and gently touching one with a finger, no matter what you've seen in the movies, is not going to do much. But jam a thumb in or poke a finger in hard, and you can inflict a lot of short, sharp pain, perfect as a distraction or in an effort to be released from someone's grip before escaping. (Which is always the ultimate aim.)

Here are a couple of easy to find points you can exploit. As always, less is more with effective techniques. Yes there are many potential pressure points on a body, but it's better to know and remember two than to half-learn and forget twenty.

If you want to understand just how nasty these feel, try testing these areas out on yourself – gently!

Clavicle/Throat Point

Look at someone from the front; you'll see the shoulders, and directly below the shoulders is an outline of the collar bones or Clavicle. These collar bones slope from the outside towards the center of the body and come together just below the neck.

Where these two bones end is a small hollow at the base of the throat – this is the target point.

In a situation where someone is facing you and perhaps holding you firmly, get a thumb and jam it into this gap and push hard. Don't worry too much about being precise; remember this isn't a fight, and getting too caught up in the specifics is just wasting time. (After all we want to be engaged for no more than 3 Seconds.)

Shove the thumb in there, and push fast and hard. This has several benefits:

- **It hurts!**
- **It triggers a natural recoil reaction (It feels terrible!)**
- **It pushes against the windpipe (Trachea) restricting breathing**
- **It is soft and will not resist your thumb**

Philtrum/Nose Point

Look at a person's face. Directly above the upper lip is the part where the two ridges rise to meet the nose. At the point where nose and face meet is the target.

This area is a particularly nasty pressure point that can stop even the most determined attacker. In life or death scenarios, you can of course strike this point with perhaps a palm heel for a devastating effect, but to take control of an opponent, you can simply wedge a finger or thumb right under the base of the nose and push their head back.

The incredible thing about this point is that while the head normally controls the body, this spot can control the head and, in turn, the rest of an individual.

Use a thumb from in front, a hooked finger from behind, or just press against it and shove with whatever you have free. The opponents head will instinctively go back since it feels so unnatural to resist pressure at this spot.

As always, once they are pushed back and distracted, make your escape.

Benefits of this point include:

- **Hard to resist. Very hard to push back against this weak point.**
- **Creates a natural recoil**
- **Controls the entire body**

Your Striking Tools

Striking tools are essentially the opposite of target zones. Where you might look for the extra weak or extra sensitive areas of an opponent's body to exploit as a target, the actual body part you use to inflict the strike must be the opposite: strong, fast, and resistant to pain.

Some of the "tools" you may use to hit an opponent are obvious, while others are less so, but the following tips offer some insight into the parts of your body already designed for dealing damage. All you have to do is use them!

Grappling

Over the years, a number of people have asked me why I don't include grappling techniques such as those found within BJJ or MMA within self-defense instruction.

I went into some detail regarding the specific reasons grappling is probably not the best choice for Self-defense earlier, but the primary concern with wrestling-style techniques is that it implies an extended period of engagement with the enemy. This is totally counter to the principle of a quick escape.

The longer you are tied up with an attacker, the more chance there is for something to go wrong and for the opponent (or their friends) to inflict serious injury.

Of course, you could end up in a tussle and locking limbs with someone even if you don't wish to, but the aim of this guide is to offer the simplest and most effective ways to neutralize an attacker in the most common situations.

Anyone, regardless of experience, can learn how to throw a palm strike to an attacker's face before running to escape, but learning a perfect "Kimura" lock is beyond most beginners and would be more likely draw them into a "fight" scenario, instead of a self-defense one.

Learning effective grappling skills is a fine goal but if pure self-defense is your aim consider looking elsewhere initially.

How to Choose the Right Tool for the Job

Techniques vs. Tools

If you read my first book, you may have seen the numerous and specific self-defense examples. These are techniques for protecting yourself against the most common methods of attack.

These are effective and simple to learn, but what happens if an aggressor approaches in a different manner? Or your defense suddenly goes wrong?

If we break down each "technique", the individual movements might best be described as tools.

So the best way to think about all the various strikes and specific physical movements is as tools in your self-defense kit.

Consider your tools as part of a set. Together, they combine to become a full and complete system, but you are also free to reach into the set and use whichever individual ones you wish depending on the threat you face.

Choosing Wisely

You can of course use whatever you want to protect yourself. After all, the only 'wrong' thing is to do nothing. But there are distinctly advantageous tools for a given situation.

Ask any tradesperson, and they will tell you of the importance of maintaining and using the right tools for the job. Sure you *can* use an adjustable spanner, but a correctly sized socket and wrench will get the job done quicker and with less effort.

The same is true of Self-defense. Our bodies are incredible things, and we have a great number of options, but using the right implement will be quicker, easier, and, in the case of self-protection, safer.

Arms vs. Legs

As a simple rule of thumb remember that arms are faster and more instinctive but legs deliver more power.

Use your arms to deflect upper body threats and attacks to the head. Don't worry about technical hand or arm positions – we are naturally programmed to protect our heads anyway.

The arms should ideally be your first consideration for striking too. They are faster, require no loss of balance and can target an opponent's head easily.

Legs, on the other hand, are not really suitable for blocking but ideal for positioning yourself to minimize the target you present to an opponent. Aim to have feet at around 45 degrees.

Feet and legs are powerful tools in counter-attacking but usually slower and easier to spot. For this reason keep any kicks low and deliver them fast. If possible combine with an upper body technique to disguise your lower body movements.

Remember to keep your legs away from danger – you will need them to run away!

About the Images

I always think it is important to include a visual reference to any topic, and self-defense is the same in this regard. Pictures are important to give us a feeling for the way a move works or the position a body should be in.

However, it's worth understanding that images, in the case of self-defense, are very much a loose guide and not the gospel of exactly how a technique should play out in real life. Violence on the street does not happen in an organized and clearly visible manner, and limbs rarely deliver clean and precise strikes.

Instead, a brief but messy scuffle is usually the order of the day, and the encounter is finished in a few seconds by decisive and positive action. This is the action that you should be taking.

For this reason, consider the instructional images within this book as a rough guide to the broad (and most important) part of any technique. I have tried to make each picture clear, but the methods are not all performed flawlessly by self-defense gurus with years of experience, because after-all, it would not be that way on the street.

Make sure to read the instructions, reference the images, and, most importantly, practice them at home or in your gym/club. It's a definite advantage to have knowledge, but the experience of movements and the feeling of performing a technique are just as essential.

The Palm Is Mightier Than the Fist

There are lots of reasons why a palm or palm-heel is usually more suitable for self-defense than a clenched fist. These have been discussed in some depth before, but, for those in doubt, here is a simple exercise you can try to demonstrate the difference in power and durability.

Remember, in the real world, there is no guarantee you will hit your target perfectly square like you may in a training hall on a focus pad. Miss with a fist, and you are likely to break fingers. A palm gives you much more room for error.

How to Test the Difference:

It's easy for me to say one technique is better than another, but let's take a look at some hard proof. This quick practical exercise demonstrates the big difference between a palm and fist.

- Find a solid vertical wall with a painted or smooth surface. (Preferably one not made of plaster or dry-wall and not one that you may accidentally punch through!)

- First, try leaning your whole body weight against the wall. Initially, just try using your palms. Note how it feels – probably not too bad.

- Now again lean against the wall, but this time using your knuckles in clenched fists. (You should already notice that the fist hurts a little more.)

STEP 2

- Stand back up straight, and position yourself facing the wall.

- With a clenched fist, **gently** strike the wall, punching the surface, and increasing the power until you reach the point of a little pain. Stop before it hurts.

- Now, repeat the strike against the wall but with an open palm. Again, stop when you reach a little pain.

- Notice the difference? You will be able to deliver much stronger blows without causing any pain through a palm strike rather than through a clenched fist.

Imagine you are using these techniques against someone in self-defense and that you have accidentally hit the forehead or a hard part of someone's body. Using a fist at full strength, you would be in agony, perhaps with broken fingers, and probably have your ability to use that hand taken away for a while. Using a palm heel, you can deliver the same, if not more power, and shake off any mistakes more easily.

Note: The point of this exercise is not to injure yourself or test how much pain you can take! It is to demonstrate the natural difference between power from a punch and a palm heel. Don't push yourself beyond the pain point.

1. How to Use Your Palm Heel

I recommend the palm-heel as the go-to striking technique in self- defense. It is powerful, fast, and comes from the relaxed, calming gesture of having both hands up. Almost any upper body area can be a target, but here are a few you may find the palm-heel especially suitable for.

Nose Strike (Potentially fatal)

The palm-heel to nose strike is utterly devastating. So much so that I only recommend this in life-or-death scenarios. If you'd rather just inflict some damage and escape, then try the jaw strike.

However, if you are in the middle of an assault situation and genuinely fear for your life, then go for it and do not hesitate.

- *With one hand raised in an open palm toward the opponent, raise the other palm, and use a hard, fast, strike into the underside of their nose. (Roughly where the nose meets the upper lip.)*

- *It is important that this technique is snapped out as a strike for maximum effect, but in close-range, you can also use it as a shove which feels equally nasty but creates less long term damage.*

Jaw Strike

The Jaw area contains the most powerful muscle in the body, the Maseter. The bone however is far more vulnerable with connections to other crucial points on the head, making it a great target for the palm heel strike.

- *Again, we use the spare hand to block with an open palm, but this time the striking hand comes up and slightly from the side. (Though do not be afraid of doing it straight to the front either.)*

- *The speed of the strike is aiming to break the jaw or incapacitate the enemy, so make it quick.*

- As always, return to guard, check your surroundings, and escape.

Chin Strike

The chin is a similar target to the jaw in that it looks strong but it can offer leverage against the entire head.

- This is a similar principal to the jaw, but this strike comes from beneath, up, and straight ahead.

- For added effect, consider pushing the opponents head back and using fingers in the eyes.

Chest Strike

A palm-heel to the chest is an excellent neutralizing strike with less risk of long term damage or worse to the attacker. As mentioned before, if you genuinely fear for your life, then don't worry about the level of risk – your life comes first. But if you are unsure of the level of danger, a short sharp strike to the chest can effectively wind an opponent and prevent them from pursuing you while also giving them a chance to fully recover in time.

- *This time, make sure you use speed combined with a twist of the hips (if you haven't already) to generate power.*

- *The aim is to strike hard and fast directly to the center of the chest, winding an opponent and preventing their ability to pursue.*

2. How to Use an Elbow

Elbows are one of the most powerful and effective strikes you can use in Self-defense. They are easily used, deliver genuine stopping power, and do not require great arm-strength to perform. (Most strength comes from the core.)

The trade-off, however, is that they are very short range and only come into play once an aggressor has entered your space. If a threat is in very close range, you will find it difficult to properly deliver a full punch, palm, or kick, and so an elbow strike can work wonders.

Elbow to Temple

The temple is the slight indentation on either side of the head. Because of its shape and reduced thickness, it offers a perfect target for a close range elbow strike to knock out or temporarily disorient an attacker.

- *Elbow strikes are close range only. Do not attempt these if you are more than arm's length away, and do not get tempted to move closer just to deliver one.*

- *Once a conflict is too close for full length palm-strikes or kicks, consider an elbow. The front arm will be easier and closer to an opponent but will be slightly less powerful.*

- *From open-hand guard, bring the front hand up and across while the elbow moves into a quick horizontal motion.*

- *Aim to strike with the strong, bony section at the tip of your forearm, not the nerve cluster further back!*

- *Twisting at the waist is crucial for generating force and speed*

Options:
- If you feel unstable or inaccurate delivering the strike, consider cupping your other hand over the fist of the striking arm as it moves and stabilizing the strike.

- If, however, you fear the opening a raised elbow may offer, you can use the other palm to cover your ribs this way.

Elbow Strike to Jaw

- *The same technique is now applied to a slightly lower target. This is more suitable if an opponent is taller than you or if their head is covered by a hat.*

- *Again, bring the elbow up from the open guard, and aim to twist into the strike bringing it parallel to their jaw.*
- *This may dislocate their bone or break some teeth, but don't stick around to find out. Once they are reeling from the strike, look around you for further danger, then escape.*

Note that in the above image the striking arm has been stabilized by the guarding hand as in the previously discussed option.

3. Using a Hammer-Fist

The simple way to understand how a hammer fist works is to think of its namesake. A hammer draws power from its rapid downward motion and delivers short sharp strikes to a small area.

You can use your fist in the same way, both striking down or sideways, particularly in situations where a normal palm-heel or fist would be ineffective or difficult to pull off.

- *From a guard position make a fist with the front hand*

- *Swing the fist using the elbow in a straight motion aiming at the temple or other direct target*

- *Hammer-Fists require the wrist to be straight and power comes from movement at the elbow joint*

- *As always, make the strike and use the distraction or temporary disorientation of the opponent to scan around and then escape*

4. How to Use the Forehead (with a Caveat)

The forehead is included here with a very important caveat. The forehead or, more specifically, a head-butt can be a very effective technique. The front part of the skull is made of some of the thickest bone in the body and, as such, can take a lot of punishment.

If an opponent tries for a punch and you duck, there is a very real chance that you will get a slight bump on the head while they leave with broken fingers.

Unfortunately, the reason this bone is so thick is due to the fact that the single most important self-defense tool you have is hidden behind it: your brain. The head needs to be protected at all costs; take a strong knock here, and it's lights out, game over. Hence, 'attacking' with the center that controls your body is a really bad idea.

So you can use the head, but only as a last resort. If you are extremely close and you do not have the ability to use elbows or knees, a quick snap of the forehead can break an attacker's nose and give you the time to escape.

- *Only consider this technique if no other options present themselves AND you are very close to an opponent*

- *Keep both hands up to protect other parts of your body. They can also be used to stabilize yourself against the attacker*

- *Thrust the head forward sharply and strike to a soft target – usually the nose – with your forehead. Do not strike with any other part of your head*

- *Once the opponent has streaming eyes or nose check around and make your escape*

5. How to Use a Knee

The knee is a powerful but short-ranged technique much like the elbow. The leg muscles are some of the largest and strongest in the body, so if you do connect with a knee strike you can successfully incapacitate an opponent quickly.

The risk of raising the knee, however, is in presenting your knee cap. As always, if you do need to strike make it quick and hard. If you leave the knee sticking out, it presents a perfect target, and someone could give you a swift kick to dislocate it.

Knee Strike to Stomach/Chest

The diaphragm and internal organs are especially susceptible to a rapid knee, and using yours against an attacker is almost guaranteed to result in them gasping for breath – if executed properly.

- *Only deliver this technique from a balanced stance, close to the opponent*

- *As always keep both hands up in an open-hand guard to initially protect yourself but also stabilize your movement (as above) since using a leg removes some stability.*

- *Quickly bring your hands to the opponents upper shoulders or neck and drive your rear leg up, bringing the knee hard into their stomach or ribs*

- *It can be difficult to deliver a knee straight up to this region. Try angling it slightly as it rises*

- *The technique can also be delivered off the front leg but this reduces power*

- *Always return to the balanced stance before making your escape*

Knee strike to the head

A knee strike to the head or face is truly devastating, but it requires a lot of movement from the defender. If at any point the attacker realizes he/she is being brought down, they may try to resist.

To counter this, make the grab and pull-down as fast as possible.

- *This time the hands grab higher at the back of the head or neck and pull down quickly*

- *Avoid interlocking your fingers. This can slow you down and cause a tangle*

- *Snap the knee up hard into the opponent's head or face*

- *Release, check around and escape*

Knee strike to groin

The groin is a famous self-defense target and the knee is brutally effective in striking it. Be aware however that in most cases a kick is safer than a Knee due to the distance required in making contact.

- *Again only consider this technique if you are very close*

- *Stabilize your balance by grasping the opponent on the shoulders*

- *Place your head slightly to the side of the attacker – not directly in front*

- *Drive the knee hard and fast into the groin region*

- *Important: Be aware this may cause a doubling over effect. Don't get headbutted!*

- *Release, scan and escape*

6. How to Use a Fist (With Caveat)

Punching with a closed fist is probably the most famous fighting technique of all time, and it does have several applications that can be effective. Unfortunately, for the uninitiated, a fist presents a special risk of broken fingers and a useless hand.

Punching to the face is a common mistake for many beginners since it is the most obvious target, but slightly miss-time your strike, and you end up hitting the forehead or other bony parts and causing yourself a lot of damage.

In most cases, an open palm-heel is just as effective and more user-friendly to the self-defense beginner, but if you are set on using punches, consider targeting soft tissue parts of the body that won't damage your hand or punish you for incorrectly positioned fingers.

Here are a couple of punches that won't (normally) result in fractured metacarpals:

Punch to the stomach

If a tussle has been going on for a few seconds and your palms have not been effective, you can mix it up once close enough and bring a fist into play by aiming lower.

Always remember that the thumb goes on the outside and that you don't need to tense the fist constantly. Stay relaxed and wait until just before the strike makes contact to tense the fist.

- *From a balanced stance keep both hands up in an open hand gesture*

- *Turn one hand into a fist (Front hand for speed, rear hand for power)*

- *Twist the fist at the same time as driving it below the ribs into the soft stomach tissue*

- *This may double over or 'wind' the attacker. Use this gap to check around and escape*

Punch to the Throat

Have you ever seen someone punched in the throat? It's quite unlikely since the technique rarely features on movies and TV, and it's a decidedly unglamorous though effective strike.

Targeting is important here. The throat is relatively small compared to a stomach or back, and it's crucial you hit it with speed and accuracy, so practice drills may be helpful.

- *From the same stance as before we have both hands up in a relaxed gesture*

- *Quickly turn one hand (front is recommended) into a fist and jab for the attacker's throat*

- *Aim for the Adam's Apple area with a fast strike to damage the windpipe*

- *Look around and make your escape*

Punch to the Kidneys

Most techniques assume that you are facing the aggressor, but fights are messy, and it's easy for people to get spun around.

- *This method follows the same technique from the previous punches but turned around to the rear*

- *Aim for the spot just below the ribs with a low punch*

- *Recover the hand back to neutral, check around for further danger and remove yourself from the scene*

7. Using Your Fingers

The fingers are a nasty tool that can inflict some serious damage, so they should only be used in dire situations. Of course, in most of the scenarios in this book, we are assuming the situation is indeed dire, but only in the worst positions should we consider blinding someone as a viable technique.

As a slight caveat, it's important to make finger strikes fast. If you leave your fingers out or show them to an opponent, they make a convenient target for them to grab and twist – which you definitely don't want!

Eye Jam

This technique is best employed if an attacker is attempting a slower-strength based attack like strangling. You can use it slowly to shove an opponent away or quick to jab as a distraction.

Be aware that the harder and quicker you push the more chance of long-term sight damage there will be. Fine if you are in genuine danger, not so fine if you are practicing with a friend.

- *If an attacker is close and attempting a sustained assault you can employ this technique*

- *When facing an opponent you bring both hands up as usual in the guard position*

- *Then push both hands up and aim to push the thumbs into the opponent's eyes*

- *You can stabilize the technique by resting the fingers on their temple or forehead but don't be afraid to shove hard and fast*

- *Once the attacker is neutralized make your escape*

Eye Claw

This technique is animalistic in approach and draws strength from its simple brutality. Optionally employed as a follow up to the palm heel strike it also allows more room for error since multiple fingers can make contact.

- *Best utilized from the front arm this strike can be delivered as part of a palm-heel to the jaw or nose*

- *From the guard position form a claw-type shape with your leading hand and strike to the face with the palm-heel*

- *After you make contact with the palm bring the fingers down quickly and grab for the eyes*

- *Jam the fingers in or scrape down. There are few rules beyond striking hard and fast!*

- *Even a small amount of contact with the eyes should bring an opponent to their knees. Take this chance to scan for other danger then escape*

Fingertip strike

The fingertip strike is very similar to the previous strike with the exception that it is used as more of a jab than a grab. It is essential that you do not keep your fingers out for longer than needed however as they can not only provide a convenient target for an attacker but also have a tendency to get caught or twisted in clothing.

- *From the open-hand guard we lead with the front (closest arm)*

- *Keep your hands in the open-palm position until you actually make the strike. Don't signal your intentions too early.*

- *When you strike jab the fingers out fast. Keep them strong but not locked out – in case you hit the forehead instead*

- *If successful use the distraction and resulting blurred vision of the attacker to escape*

8. How to Use Your Feet (with a Caveat)

Kicks are a staple of many martial arts, and while they look impressive, the real world applications are limited.

With kicks, consider this simple principle:

If you bring your foot higher than your groin, be prepared to fall.

That's not to say the opponent will always catch your leg and put you on your backside – though that is a real risk – but just like the rest of the body, our balance suffers while under stress. Flinging your legs around like Bruce Lee while panic affects your balance is more likely to make you stumble or trip, and even a slight fall can end any self-defense aspirations.

Snap kick to knee

It is crucial to keep kicks as simple and effective as possible. The snap kick is as basic as it gets and can easily be utilized by anyone wearing shoes. Essentially just a toe-poke to the knee, the aim is more of a distraction and temporary hindrance than long term injury.

Note: Do not attempt this kick barefoot or with open-toed shoes on. Most footwear has a re-enforced tip and this is the striking spot. If yours doesn't consider a different tactic.

- *Snap kicks depend on quality targeting since the toe (a small region) must strike the knee (also a small region). If you are not confident in this consider the other kicks.*

- *From your guard, or even better, after a high section technique pick up your knee*

- *Flick the toe of your shoe into the front or side of the attacker kneecap with as much force as you can manage without 'telegraphing' the move.*

- *As a guide wherever you point your knee will usually be where you kick. Point your knee at theirs for accuracy*

Groin Kick

The groin kick is one of the most famous self-defense methods for good reason; it works! However it is limited to certain applications and shouldn't be attempted unless an opponent is facing you square-on and you are sure you will connect properly. If you make the kick and miss you are unlikely to get a second chance as males are rightfully wary of the region.

The kick is slightly more advisable than the knee as it allows you to maintain a safer distance.

Naturally the technique also offers significantly less benefit when utilized against women.

- *From the 50/50 guarding position look for an opportunity when the attacker is completely facing you, not turned to one side*

- *Keeping the hands up raise your knee to point at just above their groin region*

- *Kick out hard and fast towards where your knee is pointing. Make it count! (Either leg can be used)*

- *Aim to strike in a rising motion with the lace-portion of your shoe, which gives a larger striking area*

- *Note: All the kicking steps should be undertaken as fast as accurately possible to prevent the opponent turning*

- *They may double over in pain. Make sure you don't get caught with this then make your escape*

Shin Kick

The shin kick is unique in that in can be a kick –snapped out to strike the bone or it can be pushed against the shin and scraped down – or a combination of the two as dictated by your circumstances.

For this reason it works well at kicking distance but also if someone is close or holding on to you.

- *From the guard position raise your knee to point at their knee*

- *The front or back leg can be used but the rear leg usually offers more power and ease of movement*

- *Twist your foot so your toes are slightly pointing out at around 30 degrees*

- *Stamp the instep (where the sole meets the inside of your foot) into the attacker's shin bone*

- *The natural curve of your foot should lend itself to 'wrap' slightly around it*

- *Either strike hard and remove or also scrape the foot down hard across the bone*

- *If the opponent is in pain but still standing shove them away hard, check for other danger and run. They should have difficulty pursuing.*

- *As always these movements are performed hard and fast*

9. Special Mention: Throat Jam

The throat jam is a unique technique that works extremely well in one spot but is not really recommended for use anywhere else. Because the throat is mainly soft tissue and a great spot to quickly disable an attacker, we use this technique quickly to create a window of escape.

Open your first finger and thumb and look for the V-shaped gap between them. This is the striking region. Because of its unique shape, it is perfectly designed for a short, sharp jab to the throat of an aggressor.

Despite how it may look the Throat Jam is actually a fast strike, like a punch, not a strangling motion.

- *From an open-hand, guarding block, simply stiffen up one hand and bring the thumb out to one side.*

- *You can choose the front hand for speed, or if closer the rear hand for power, but always leave another hand free for protection.*

- *Jab the V shape made with your hand hard and fast into the front of the attacker's throat. (On men, aim for the Adam's Apple).*

- *If done fast enough, they should suffer bruising and a partially collapsed trachea making it temporarily difficult for them to breathe.*

- *Arms up, check your surroundings, and make an exit.*

Weapons Defenses

Weapons are actually rarely used in a "fight" situation on the street; more commonly, they are deployed as tools of intimidation to coerce or threaten a target into giving up. That said, you shouldn't take the presence of a weapon lightly.

The most likely cause of injury from weapons in a self-defense arena is from a botched block, counter-attack, or scuffle. Most attackers are not skilled in their use or control of blades and/or firearms. Because of this, it is more likely that a mistake will cause injury to you (or them) than the intentional use of said weapon.

As always, if threatened by a thief with a weapon, try to hand over the money, phone, or whatever the aggressor is after. It is only if we still fear for our life or an unprovoked attack arises that we consider physical action.

If you live in an area with numerous reports of weapon based crime consider looking into specific weapon-defense courses in your area and investing in dedicated reading materials – or if possible, move!

The following chapters are principle foundations for protection against the most common weapons.

Principles of Gun Defense

The biggest danger around firearms is also the greatest advantage. It is incredibly easy to shoot someone if you wish to. An attacker sneaking up on you could probably fire before you even knew about it. Luckily, for this same reason, if you find yourself facing a gun, it is unlikely the aggressor actually wants to shoot you or he/she would have done so already.

Remember, in this scenario that they are using the firearm as a tool for intimidation, a tool for getting your money, or just a tool to help them feel tough. In most situations like this, it is perfectly fine to just hand over your money and try to keep the situation calm. Placating phrases like "OK" or "That's fine" in an even voice help keep things under control.

In a firearm encounter, you do not want to aggravate the aggressor unnecessarily. This is the same for any weapon attack of course, but a street thug bearing a gun is unlikely to have the trigger discipline worthy of the weapon. This could lead to unwanted discharges and a complete loss of control over the situation, leading not only to potential personal injury but also injury to passers-by.

Only engage a person wielding a gun as a last resort if, after all other efforts, you still fear for your life.

Priorities in firearm defense

1. Remove yourself from the line of fire
2. Remove the attacker's ability to fire and/or pursue
3. Escape the scene quickly

Principles of Bats / Swung Weapon Defense

Despite looking scary, bats, batons, and swung weapons aren't really an ideal weapon for attacking someone. They require a big wind up to do any damage – which can be easily spotted – and the actual point of impact is quite small. If you are either too close or too far from the attacker, a bat is quite useless.

This is the basis for any defense from a swung weapon. Either; get very close and disarm them, or get just out of range and run. If an attacker decides to give chase, carrying a swung weapon will slow them down considerably.

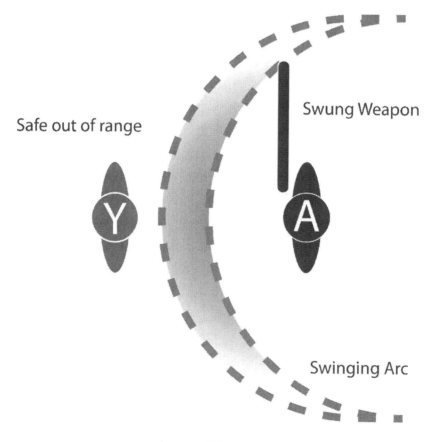

Safe out of range

Swung Weapon

Swinging Arc

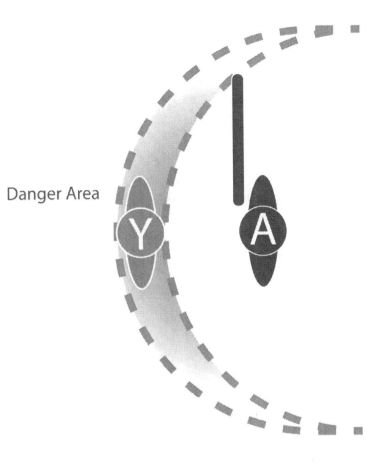

Danger Area

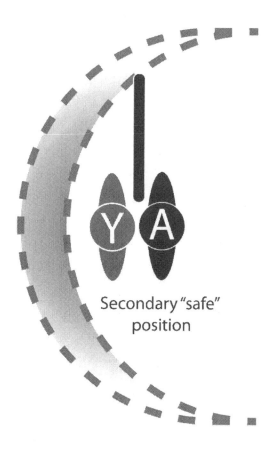

Secondary "safe" position

Principles of Blade Defense

I've said it before, and I'll say it again. Don't carry a knife for defense unless you are prepared to get stabbed by it. Only a fool carries an offensive weapon that an opponent might easily be able to use against you.

But what if someone pulls a blade on you?

Firstly of course, unless you fear for your life, just hand over the wallet, phone, or whatever they are after.

Unlike bats, getting close will not help you here. In fact, quite the opposite. Establishing a good distance is essential in knife defense. Yes, we've seen the movies where someone can throw a knife and kill a man at 50 feet, but in reality, this skill is incredibly rare. Someone carrying a bladed weapon is unlikely to throw it away intentionally, and even a small mistake would give you the blade instead of them.

Blades are similar to guns in that, if an attacker is flashing one around in front of you, it is usually as an intimidation tool – rather than an assault one. If an attacker really wanted to stab you, chances are you wouldn't see or hear it until after the event.

Don't be scared by this prospect even though it sounds worrying. Unwarranted stabbings do happen, but they are rare. The only case where this becomes more likely is if you are involved in regular violence or gang culture, in which case you should probably reconsider your choices anyway.

Visible attacks with a knife usually occur after either a botched defense attempt or when a situation has escalated and anger brings out weapons. This is why we advocate a "de-escalation and run" priority before any engagement!

Cross-slashes and stabs are the danger in a knife encounter, and as such, so long as you remain out of arm's length, you are relatively safe.

- Stay out of range of the blade where possible and calm the situation down

- If you do need to deflect a knife try to keep it as far away from your body and major organs as possible

- If a scuffle occurs it's likely, no matter how careful you are that both parties will get cut at some point. Try not to panic if this happens and seek medical assistance once you have escaped the scene

- Do NOT carry an offensive knife yourself. (Many people trip and fall on their own blades during an altercation)

No Slashers

It's also worth pointing out that despite what you see in horror movies, attackers almost never hold a knife over their head and charge with a slashing downward motion. You can learn defenses against it if you wish, but it is unlikely you would ever see this on the street.

How to Avoid the No.1 Striking Mistake: The Importance of Recovery

This isn't recovery from injury – although that is important – or what to do when things have gone wrong – which was covered in the previous book. No, instead we are talking about recovering your position after a strike, which is an often overlooked yet crucial principle of physical defense.

Think about it: we get psyched up and prepare ourselves to deliver a devastating strike to incapacitate our opponent and make him think twice about causing trouble again.

"Oh yeah this guy is going down in one hit. I will escape and tell all my friends about how I defeated this mugger."

So you wind up and put everything you have into the palm-heel. Powered by the gods themselves, you know the energy coursing through your hand would stop a freight train.

And then you miss.

What now?

Do you try another strike? Run away? Cry?

Instead, consider setting yourself up correctly right from the start.

50/50

Lots of martial arts discuss the pros and cons of fighting stances and correct weight distribution, but for our purposes, we want to keep it as simple as possible. 50/50 balance is the easiest and most effective stance to begin from, giving you a good range of strikes, defenses, and a solid foundation.

- Place feet approximately shoulder width apart.

- Put roughly equal weight on the front and back legs.
- Turn the feet and body to about 45 degrees while still facing the front (to present less of a target).
- Most importantly, always ensure you can return to this position quickly.

It might mean you need fairly quick reactions to return to 50/50, but the other essential principle is to keep your techniques "tight" and not overcompensate.

"Err on the side of caution."

We always assume the opponent is strong, fast, and could take our legs away. This 50/50 stance gives you the most stable position and the least likelihood of being tripped. We also try to never over-reach with a technique. Short, sharp, and powerful is far safer than winding up some monumental haymaker that risks throwing you across the room.

Consider the smallest possible movement you need to make to achieve your goal, and aim for that.

How to Develop Natural Body Armor

When most people think of "tough" guys or individuals that would be good in a fight, the first images that spring to mind are huge, muscular, rough-looking sorts probably covered in scars or tattoos. While the majority of this stereotype is complete fantasy, one area does actually help your body defend itself easier.

Fitness is the first line of defense, as we've already explored in my first book. Being physically able to run, escape, or defend yourself without collapsing in a wheezing heap is far more important than learning some fiddly arm lock that you may never use.

But similarly, the composition of your physical body can make a big difference to your ability to protect the vital organs.

Muscle is denser than fat and offers greater resistance to impact and trauma. By building muscle definition, we can effectively create a layer of protective tissue around the sensitive parts of our body.

Muscles: Natures body armor

Worried about getting hit in the belly? Abdominal exercises can help you develop these muscles and offer protection to the soft tissue.

Concerned you might fall on your back? Back raises stretch and strengthen the lower back muscles, including the Erector Spinae – the muscles that run up either side of your spine. Perfect these to protect the delicate nervous system.

Interested in being able to block effectively? Building up arm and leg strength will give you the muscle tone to greatly improve deflection of impact.

Be Functionally Fit

Now with this in mind, you may be tempted to chug a few protein shakes and hit the heavy weights down the gym, and there is nothing wrong with this per se. There does come a point, however, in muscle building where we pass healthy, functional fitness and head into muscles for show, the kind seen on many body builders.

Despite their appearance and impressive dedication to the gym, body builders aren't particularly efficient at Martial Arts or self-defense. Because they have such incredible muscle mass, it causes a bulking up effect that slows them down and limits their movement.

Try to watch a huge body builder sprinting, and you will see the difficulty they face when quadriceps get so big that they stop the legs from moving properly.

The same is true for self-protection. Hitting the gym and getting fit is admirable. Building muscle is great. But once you start to get "big", you are limiting your natural ability and reaction speed.

Functional fitness is more about being in the best shape for life, not for show. It is focused on a balanced approach to working out whereby you include some cardio, some weight work, some endurance training, and of course ideally some practice of punching, kicking, or striking.

If life calls upon you to suddenly run 1.5 miles, could you do it?

What about if you had to get up off the ground quickly; would it be manageable?

Could you strike someone hard a couple of times, escape quickly, and still have breath left to defend yourself?

These are the questions we aim to answer in functional fitness, and a balanced workout routine helps establish this.

Your Functional Fitness Self-Defense Workout

Not everyone is interested in working out to improve their self-defense skills and understanding the principles in this book alone will go a long way to help improve your ability, but if you are interested in taking things a little further this short exercise plan can really pay off.

With functional fitness in mind, here is a simple routine designed to work the entire body in a very short time. Couple this with some plyometric exercise for explosive power and a little extra cardio work, and you will be well prepared for the physical fitness elements of self-defense, without having to spend hours at a gym or martial arts club.

I always recommend cardio vascular endurance and core strength work as starting points within self-defense training. Being able to run a medium distance and having the power left to deliver decent strikes is far more useful than learning to bench press huge weights or run a marathon. (Although don't avoid these if they are what you enjoy!)

As always, regularity is paramount for long term effectiveness in any routine. Fitness is about regular exercise in small manageable amounts, rather than occasional insane workouts. The following is only a guideline and the number of repetitions can be reduced or increased based on your ability.

Your Self-Defense Workout:

The following routine is based on a beginner level with a combination of self-defense and fitness drills. If you already have a good baseline of fitness, you can increase the numbers or add weights to enhance the challenge.

Cardio exercise:

To make things more efficient, your warm up and Cardio exercises can be rolled into one. Aim to complete at least a half mile jog at an average pace. Or mix things up with some cycling and swimming too.

Don't kill yourself with the Cardio work. Save something for the rest of the workout.

Strength exercises:

Standing Squats

Building the foundation of power through our legs, squats are a great exercise. If you are a beginner, you can learn these with just your bodyweight. If you are a little stronger, consider adding weights at the gym.
Perform 3 sets of 15 to 20 reps

Push Ups

It's hard to go wrong with push-ups. They develop chest, shoulder, and arm strength and are so simple they can be included in any routine.
3 sets of 25-30 reps

Crunches or Sit Ups

Developing strength in the abdominal region not only helps you deliver more power in a strike but also builds muscle allowing you to resist more damage.
4 sets of 20-35 reps

Oblique Crunches

Often overlooked, the Obliques form another stabilizing section of your core and again help in delivering a solid foundation.
3 sets of 15-25 reps

Back Raises

People are quick to focus on the front of the body's muscles, but the "core" makes up the entire central region — front and back. Back raises are an easy way to develop strength in an often overlooked area.

4 sets of 15-25 reps

Plyometrics:

Martial Artists have used plyometric exercises for years to build up explosive power. You can use them as an addition to or instead of your strength drills.

You can find numerous examples in the free book from my site: www.BlackBeltFit.com

When to Hand Over the Money, When to Fight Back

So we've looked at some potential targets and techniques on an attacker. But how do we know when/if we should use them?

As we established in my first book, in almost any mugging scenario the smart move is to simply hand over your money, phone, bag, or whatever, and let the thief get what they came for and leave. It is far better to lose a few dollars or your phone than to risk your life. (Besides you can lock-out credit cards and phone's almost immediately anyway.)

Acting tough and aggravating an aggressor will not help if they just want your cash. It is most likely the mugger is seeking some easy money; give it to them, and they will leave and you can go about your day, shaken perhaps, but uninjured. Escalating the situation is bad for you and them.

So how do we know if engaging an opponent is the right choice?

There are a couple of scenarios that signal more than a simple mugging. In these cases, it is advised that you make a quick decision to escape, if necessary by physically engaging the opponent.

- **They want to take you somewhere**

This should be a big signal of impending danger, especially for women. A mugger just wants objects of value; if they have intentions of moving you somewhere, there's a good chance they want something worse.

Offer the cash and toss the wallet/purse on the ground a few feet away. As they go to retrieve it, just run.

If they are forcing you towards a car, alleyway, or side street pick your moment and make some noise while striking them hard and fast, then bolt.

- **They don't leave after getting your money or valuables**

It's important to try to remain calm while a mugger takes your money even if you don't feel it. Using calming phrases like "That's fine" or "OK" will help you feel in control and them not feel threatened. Using the open-palm guard is also important in this.

If you cower and start to show excessive fear or terror, it can empower them, and the more sinister attacker may see it as a signal to push things further. If they have taken your items but continue to hang around, perhaps getting closer, it's a signal to act. Again, pick a moment and go loud, strike, and escape.

How to 'Go Loud'

The meek might inherit the earth, but they will struggle in a self-defense situation when things go bad. It's fine, nay, good to be calm and passive when things get a bit scary in life and to not overreact, but there comes a point where you have to flip the switch and turn 'it' on.

As we've just explored, there is a moment when you have done everything you reasonably can to calm a situation down or prevent violence, but the attacker has persisted, and you have a genuine fear for your life and safety. This is when you should **'go loud'**.

Going loud means you quickly change from being calm and mild to suddenly very noisy and very physical in your efforts to protect yourself and leave the danger. This doesn't mean you turn into a nut-job; you are still very much in control, but the contrast is night and day. The idea of flipping a switch is important because we are aiming to disorient an opponent as much as possible.

Making the change quickly and suddenly throws off most people, and there will be several seconds of confusion while they figure out how to react. This is your gap to counter attack if needed and run.

If, however, you gradually get more and more loud and aggressive, the opponent has time to adjust and will see you as more of an annoyance than anything.

What do I say?

Many people are embarrassed by the idea of suddenly becoming loud and physical, but you shouldn't be. Any mugger or violent individual should be embarrassed for their actions, not you.

You can of course shout whatever you want, but suddenly yelling expletives isn't as effective as shouting for what you want. Think about it. If a friend of yours suddenly started screaming for you to "STOP WALKING!" your first instinct is to slightly panic and do exactly that, even if you eventually overcome it and carry on.

The same is true here. When you shout, make it clear what you want to happen.

Examples include:

"BACK OFF!"
"LEAVE ME ALONE!"
"STOP!"
"NO!"

If this is accompanied by a sharp strike or shove, it is an effective deterrent and also serves to bring attention to your position for any passers-by, which is exactly what most aggressors don't want.

Practice your voice with pressure testing:

An easy way to become confident using your voice in a commanding manner is to practice it over and over until you no longer think twice about it.

The following exercise works well as part of a group or class scenario but can also be practiced with just one other friend in a living room or garden.

- Find a friend or partner and large area with plenty of space to move.

- One person decides to be the 'Attacker' while the other becomes the 'Defender'. (Note that we don't use the word victim since you are never a victim if you don't wish to be.)

- The Defender will stand with their eyes closed in the center of the space, arms raised in an open hand guarding block.

- The Attacker now chooses to approach from any direction and touches the Defender on the shoulder, arm, or head for example.

- This is the signal for the Defender to respond. The Defender quickly opens his or her eyes, pushes the Attacker back firmly, and loudly says "GET BACK!" or something similar.

- Repeat this motion from multiple angles, and keep the voice firm and confident. Remember this is an exercise; you can be as loud as you want.

- Once one person has tried this a few times, swap roles, and see what it is like from the other side.

- Repeat this exercise over multiple days to get used to the experience.

Defenders: Be prepared to turn to face the Attacker. Threats can come from any angle.

Attackers: If you don't believe the Defender's voice was commanding enough, tell your friend. There is no point being nice and not helping them develop. The sharp, loud command should make you feel a little uncomfortable – this is a sign it is effective!

The Importance of Positive Focus

In closing of this book I wanted to address the flipside of self-defense preparation and that is hypervigilance. This is a condition whereby individuals become anxious and overly paranoid about their surroundings, often becoming suspicious of others.

Learning simple, effective principles for self-defense is a fine goal. It's smart to be prepared and know how to handle yourself in a tight spot.

But in my many years involved with Martial Arts and Self-protection, I have also seen a number of people who end up going the opposite direction and inadvertently start to draw danger into their life without knowing it.

In our lives, we want to avoid stress as much as possible. Reducing the odds of injury through violence is an important part of that, but if you start to obsess over danger and potential threats, it can be easy to focus on the wrong areas.

Once this happens, people can start to get unrealistically (Hyper) vigilant.

Maybe they start buying self-defense tools or weapons. Perhaps they become scared of going out, or they walk around suspecting everyone and acting furtively. The irony is of course that being over paranoid or stressed just makes you appear as more of a target and makes you stick out.

I'm here to tell you that this is not being prepared. This is being obsessed and is not productive. Try to relax, and don't worry.

If something bad has ever happened to you then that is unfortunate but never be afraid of seeking professional help – in whatever form that takes. The mind is just as fragile as the body and there are some fantastic people out there who can help you rebuild both the physical and mental self. It helped me, and it can help you too.

Luckily violence is actually quite rare in life, and most of us will never encounter any genuine threats. You are statistically at more danger from flying champagne corks (no really) or tripping on your own pants (seriously) than some deranged psycho attacking you on the street. Violence *can* happen, so a little knowledge goes a long way, but enjoying your life should always come first. This is the real key to beating any threat.

Never let fear rule you and enjoy your life. It will probably never happen!

Thank You (And a Free Book!)

I can't stress enough that any real life or death encounter will probably not go to plan, and most of the techniques you see here (or anywhere else) will be forgotten. Trust in your instinct, and never be afraid to run. If you can't run, then try to calm the situation; if the attacker wants your money, hand it over – it's only money.

It's only after all of this and if you still genuinely fear for your safety that you should start to think about blocks and counter attacks. They are always a last resort.

Thanks to Adam, Adam, and Steve for helping me put this book together and of course thanks to you for reading it! I work hard to create useful and easy to follow guides for Martial Arts, Fitness, and Self Defense. I hope you never have to use this one!

Given that you now have a better understanding of self-protection, please help others, and give this book a review if you found it useful. Positive reviews make a world of difference to authors and other readers alike. Finally, for your **COMPLETELY FREE** guide, check out my site at: www.BlackBeltFit.com

Thanks again.
- *Phil*

Other Books by Phil Pierce

Check out some of the other Martial Arts, Fitness, and Well-Being titles from Phil Pierce:

The Original and No. 1 Self Defense Bestseller:

How to Defend Yourself in 3 Seconds (or Less): The Self Defense Secrets You Need to Know! (Part 1)

http://bit.ly/1hiFSDE

With most violent encounters, the ability to defend yourself comes down to a matter of seconds where the right actions can be the difference between life and death.

Developed with input from Top Martial Artists and Self Defense experts, this illustrated guide reveals the secrets of real Self Defense and exposes the truth behind street violence.

It is designed to give you straight-forward, practical advice and keep you safe when it counts...

Fitness Hacks: 50 Shortcuts to Effortlessly Cheat Your Way to a Better Body Today!

http://bit.ly/OHpkcr

Discover 50 Simple Shortcuts for more motivation, losing fat, building muscle, and a healthier, happier body today!

'Fitness Hacks' reveals the powerful secret tips and tricks YOU can easily use in your daily life to Lose Weight, Build Muscle, or get fit fast! This expert guide, with insights from top instructors, fitness coaches, and cutting-edge research skips the BS and hard work and exposes the efficiency shortcuts and psychological "hacks" you can use right now to improve your body today!

How to Meditate in Just 2 Minutes: Easy Meditation for Beginners and Experts Alike

http://bit.ly/1dYjnz6

Given, Meditation can be an incredibly powerful tool in improving both physical and mental health, focus, and relaxation, but most people think it takes a long time to see results. The truth is, it doesn't!

With this easy-to-use book, you can quickly learn how to achieve these incredible benefits in just 2 Minutes a day…

48564525R00085

Made in the USA
Lexington, KY
05 January 2016